Basic troubleshooting for any Kindle.

Hello too all the millions of Amazon Kindle users. Kindle is a great produc
I made this e book to make it easier for all the Kindle users out there to trou
Amazon Kindle support which does a awesome job but whose wants to spe
book will cover from the first gen kindle up to the new Kindle fire 8.9 HDX. 1
wireless issues, apps issues and much more so lets

E Ink Devices

Kindle (1st Generation)

Kindle(2nd Generation)

Kindle DX

Kindle Keyboard

Kindle Touch

Kindle

Kindle Paper-White

Tablets Devices

Kindle Fire (1st Generation)

Kindle Fire (2nd Generation)

Kindle Fire HD 7"

Kindle Fire HD 8.9"

Kindle Fire HDX 7"

Kindle Fire HDX 8.9"

A Little Information To Know

Before doing any trouble shooting on your devices make sure the battery is charged up to at least 40% or more.
The number to Kindle support is 1-866-321-8851

Before resetting your device to factory default settings contact Kindle support so they can get information off the device in case further troubleshooting is needed.

When doing a hard reset of the device hold the power button for at least 30 – 45 seconds to make sure the device resets.

You want to make sure your Kindle always has the most recent software updates. Use the help pages on www.amazon.com to see if you have the most recent updates.

With some wireless issues make sure you have the correct password sometimes they can be enter wrong so just double check to be sure. If you see a white x next to the wifi symbol that means that there is a issue with your router. Kindle support can not troubleshoot routers you much contact the company or person who install it for you to check the settings in the router.

Kindle (1st Generation)

Screen Issues

Device has a image stuck on the screen or lines running across or up and down the screen This could mean screen damaged that cant be fixed

Troubleshooting

A. Try to hard reset the device by sliding the case off the back of the device getting a paperclip or something small

and press the button for 30-45 seconds then releasing the button with the device unplug for the charger then let the device reboot and see if you still have the issue.

B. Try to hard reset the device by by sliding the case off the back of the device getting a paperclip or something small and press the button for 30-45 seconds then releasing the button with the device plug into the charger then let the device reboot and see if you still have the issue.

C. Make sure your device is up to date on it's software. From the home screen hit Menu and then settings, on the bottom right of the screen you will see the Kindle version your device has. Check on www.amazon.com on the help pages to make sure you have the most updated software.

D. If this does not fix your issue contact Kindle Support. 1-866-321-8851

Charging Issues

Device will not hold a charge or shows no signs of charging.

Troubleshooting

A. Try to hard reset the device by sliding the case off the back of the device getting a paperclip or something small and press the button for 30-45 seconds then releasing the button with the device unplug for the charger then let the device reboot and see if you still have the issue.

B. Try to hard reset the device by sliding the case off the back of the device getting a paperclip or something small and press the button for 30-45 seconds then releasing the button with the device plug into the charger then let the device reboot and see if you still have the issue.

C. Make sure your device is up to date on it's software. From the home screen hit Menu and then settings, on the bottom right of the screen you will see the Kindle version your device has. Check on www.amazon.com on the help pages to make sure you have the most updated software.

D. If this does not fix your issue contact Kindle Support. 1-866-321-8851

Downloading Issues

Books or purchases does not show up on your device.

Troubleshooting

A. Make sure your order has when through and it is paid for. Orders can be put into a pending status which can take up to 4 hours to clear. Also make sure you are purchasing the items on the correct account. Customers with multiple accounts can purchases item on the account their devices are not register too which they can not get the books onto their devices.

B. Make sure your device has a good connection where your purchases can download.

C. You can go and log on to your account at www.amazon.com and go to Manage Your Kindle and see if the purchase show up in your library and send it to your device from there.

D. Try to hard reset the device by sliding the case off the back of the device getting a paperclip or something small and press the button for 30-45 seconds then releasing the button then let the device reboot and see if you still have the issue.

E. Make sure your device is up to date on it's software. From the home screen hit Menu and then settings, on the bottom right of the screen you will see the Kindle version your device has. Check on www.amazon.com on the help pages to make sure you have the most updated software.

Wireless Issues

If you device can not connect to a wireless network.

Troubleshooting

A. If you have difficulty connecting to the Kindle store or other wireless resources on your Kindle, make sure the wireless switch on the back of your Kindle 1st Generation is in the "ON" position and your battery is charged.

B. Make sure your network has a good connection Call your isp to make sure there is no outages in you area.

C. Try to hard reset the device by sliding the case off the back of the device getting a paperclip or something small and press the button for 30-45 seconds then releasing the button then let the device reboot and see if you still have the issue.

D. Make sure your device is up to date on it's software. From the home screen hit Menu and then settings, on the bottom right of the screen you will see the Kindle version your device has. Check on

www.amazon.com on the help pages to make sure you have the most updated software.

E. De-register and the re-register the Kindle then do a hard reset the device by sliding the case off the back of the device getting a paperclip or something small and press the button for 30-45 seconds then releasing the button then let the device reboot and try to connect to your network. If you still have the issue. Go to a local place that providers free wifi and see if you can connect there to rule out if there is anything wrong with your connection at home or work.

F. Reset to factory Default but not recommended until you contact Kindle support so they can get information off the device in case further

troubleshooting is needed. 1-866-321-8851

G If you see a white x next to the wifi that means that there is a issue with your router. Kindle support can not troubleshoot routers you much contact the company or person who install it for you to check the settings in the router.

Kindle (2nd Generation)

Screen Issues

Device has a image stuck on the screen or lines running across or up and down the screen This could mean screen damaged that cant be fixed

Troubleshooting

A. Try to hard reset the device by sliding the power button for 30-45 seconds then releasing the button with the device unplug for the charger then let the device reboot and see if you still have the issue.

B. Try to hard reset the device by sliding the power button for 30-45 seconds then releasing the button with the device plug into the charger then let the device reboot and see if you still have the issue.

C. Make sure your device is up to date on it's software. From the home screen hit Menu and then settings, on the bottom right of the screen you will see the Kindle version your device has. Check on www.amazon.com on the help pages to make sure you have the most updated software.

D. If this does not fix your issue contact Kindle Support. 1-866-321-8851

Charging Issues

Device will not hold a charge or shows no signs of charging.

Troubleshooting

A. Try to hard reset the device by sliding the power button for 30-45 seconds then releasing the button with the device unplug for the charger then let the device reboot and see if you still have the issue.

B. Try to hard reset the device by sliding the power button for 30-45 seconds then releasing the button with the device plug into the charger then let the device reboot and see if you still have the issue.

C. Make sure your device is up to date on it's software. From the home screen hit Menu and then settings, on the bottom right of the screen you will see the Kindle version your device has. Check on www.amazon.com on the help pages to make sure you have the most updated software.

D. If this does not fix your issue contact Kindle Support. 1-866-321-8851

Downloading Issues

Books or purchases does not show up on your device.

Troubleshooting

A. Make sure your order has when through and it is paid for. Orders can be put into a pending status which can take up to 4 hours to clear. Also make sure you are purchasing the items on the correct account. Customers with multiple accounts can purchases item on the account their

devices are not register too which they can not get the books onto their devices.

B. Make sure your device has a good connection where your purchases can download.

C. You can go and log on to your account at www.amazon.com and go to Manage Your Kindle and see if the purchase show up in your library and send it to your device from there.

D. Try to hard reset the device by sliding the power button for 30-45 seconds then releasing the button, then let the device reboot and see if you still have the issue.

E. Make sure your device is up to date on it's software. From the home screen hit Menu and then settings, on the bottom right of the screen you will see the Kindle version your device has. Check on www.amazon.com on the help pages to make sure you have the most updated software.

F. If this does not fix your issue contact Kindle Support. 1-866-321-8851

Wireless Issues

If you device can not connect to a wireless network.

Troubleshooting

A. If you have difficulty connecting to the Kindle store or other wireless resources on your Kindle, make sure the wireless switch on the back of your Kindle 1st Generation is in the "ON" position and your battery is charged.

B. Make sure your network has a good connection Call your isp to make sure there is no outages in you area.

C. Try to hard reset the device by sliding the power button for 30-45 seconds then releasing the button then let the device reboot and see if you still have the issue.

D. Make sure your device is up to date on it's software. From the home screen hit Menu and then settings, on the bottom right of the screen you will see the Kindle version your device has. Check on www.amazon.com on the help pages to make sure you have the most updated software.

E. De-register and the re-register the Kindle then do a hard reset then let the device reboot and try to connect to your network. If you still have the issue. Go to a local place that providers free wifi and see if you can connect there to rule out if there is anything wrong with your connection at home or work.

F. Reset to factory Default but not recommended until you contact Kindle support so they can get information off the device in case further troubleshooting is needed. 1-866-321-8851

G. If you see a white x next to the wifi that means that there is a issue with your router. Kindle support can not troubleshoot routers you much contact the company or person who install it for you to check the settings in the router.

Kindle DX

Screen Issues

Device has a image stuck on the screen or lines running across or up and down the screen This could mean screen damaged that cant be fixed

Troubleshooting

A. Try to hard reset the device by sliding the power button for 30-45 seconds then releasing the button with the device unplug for the charger then let the device reboot and see if you still have the issue.

B. Try to hard reset the device by sliding the power button for 30-45 seconds then releasing the button with the device plug into the charger then let the device reboot and see if you still have the issue.

C. Make sure your device is up to date on it's software. From the home screen hit Menu and then settings, on the bottom right of the screen you will see the Kindle version your device has. Check on www.amazon.com on the help pages to make sure you have the most updated software.

D. If this does not fix your issue contact Kindle Support. 1-866-321-8851

Charging Issues

Device will not hold a charge or shows no signs of charging.

Troubleshooting

A. Try to hard reset the device by sliding the power button for 30-45 seconds then releasing the button with the device unplug for the charger then let the device reboot and see if you still have the issue.

B. Try to hard reset the device by sliding the power button for 30-45 seconds then releasing the button with the device plug into the charger then let the device reboot and see if you still have the issue.

C. Make sure your device is up to date on it's software. From the home screen hit Menu and then settings, on the bottom right of the screen you will see the Kindle version your device has. Check on www.amazon.com on the help pages to make sure you have the most updated software.

D. If this does not fix your issue contact Kindle Support. 1-866-321-8851

Downloading Issues

Books or purchases does not show up on your device.

Troubleshooting

A. Make sure your order has when through and it is paid for. Orders can be put into a pending status which can take up to 4 hours to clear. Also make sure you are purchasing the items on the correct account. Customers with multiple accounts can purchases item on the account their devices are not register too which they can not get the books onto their devices.

B. Make sure your device has a good connection where your purchases can download.

C. You can go and log on to your account at www.amazon.com and go to Manage Your Kindle and see if the purchase show up in your library and send it to your device from there.

D. Try to hard reset the device by sliding the power button for 30-45 seconds then releasing the button then let the device reboot and see if you still have the issue.

E. Make sure your device is up to date on it's software. From the home screen hit Menu and then settings, on the bottom right of the screen you will see the Kindle version your device has. Check on www.amazon.com on the help pages to make sure you have the most updated software.

F. If this does not fix your issue contact Kindle Support. 1-866-321-8851

Wireless Issues

If you device can not connect to a wireless network.

Troubleshooting

A. If you have difficulty connecting to the Kindle store or other wireless resources on your Kindle, make sure the wireless switch on the back of your Kindle 1st Generation is in the "ON" position and your battery is charged.

B. Make sure your network has a good connection Call your isp to make sure there is no outages in you area.

C. Try to hard reset the device by sliding the power button for 30-45 seconds then releasing the button then let the device reboot and see if you still have the issue.

D. Make sure your device is up to date on it's software. From the home screen hit Menu and then settings, on the bottom right of the screen you will see the Kindle version your device has. Check on www.amazon.com on the help pages to make sure you have the most updated software.

E. De-register and the re-register the Kindle then do a hard reset then let the device reboot and try to connect to your network. If you still have the issue. Go to a local place that providers free wifi and see if you can connect there to rule out if there is anything wrong with your connection at home or work.

F. Reset to factory Default but not recommended until you contact Kindle support so they can get information off the device in case further troubleshooting is needed. 1-866-321-8851

Kindle Keyboard

Screen Issues

Device has a image stuck on the screen or lines running across or up and down the screen This could mean screen damaged that cant be fixed

Troubleshooting

A. Try to hard reset the device by sliding the power button for 30-45 seconds then releasing the button with the device unplug for the charger then let the device reboot and see if you still have the issue.

B. Try to hard reset the device by sliding the power button for 30-45 seconds then releasing the button with the device plug into the charger then let the device reboot and see if you still have the issue.

C. Make sure your device is up to date on it's software. From the home screen hit Menu and then settings, on the bottom right of the screen you will see the Kindle version your device has. Check on www.amazon.com on the help pages to make sure you have the most updated software.

D. If this does not fix your issue contact Kindle Support. 1-866-321-8851

Charging Issues

Device will not hold a charge or shows no signs of charging.

Troubleshooting

A. Try to hard reset the device by sliding the power button for 30-45 seconds then releasing the button with the device unplug for the charger then let the device reboot and see if you still have the issue.

B. Try to hard reset the device by sliding the power button for 30-45 seconds then releasing the button with the device plug into the charger then let the device reboot and see if you still have the issue.

C. Make sure your device is up to date on it's software. From the home screen hit Menu and then settings, on the bottom right of the screen you will see the Kindle version your device has. Check on www.amazon.com on the help pages to make sure you have the most updated software.

D. If this does not fix your issue contact Kindle Support. 1-866-321-8851

Downloading Issues

Books or purchases does not show up on your device.

A. Make sure your order has when through and it is paid for. Orders can be put into a pending status which can take up to 4 hours to clear. Also make sure you are purchasing the items on the correct account. Customers with multiple accounts can purchases item on the account their devices are not register too which they can not get the books onto their devices.

B. Make sure your device has a good connection where your purchases can download.

C. You can go and log on to your account at www.amazon.com and go to Manage Your Kindle and see if the purchase show up in your library and send it to your device from there.

D. Try to hard reset the device by sliding the power button for 30-45 seconds then releasing the button then let the device reboot and see if you still have the issue.

E. Make sure your device is up to date on it's software. From the home screen hit Menu and then settings, on the bottom right of the screen you will see the Kindle version your device has. Check on www.amazon.com on the help pages to make sure you have the most updated software.

F. If this does not fix your issue contact Kindle Support. 1-866-321-8851

Wireless Issues

If you device can not connect to a wireless network.

Troubleshooting

A. If you have difficulty connecting to the Kindle store or other wireless resources on your Kindle, make sure the wireless switch on the back of your Kindle 1st Generation is in the "ON" position and your battery is charged.

B. Make sure your network has a good connection Call your isp to make sure there is no outages in you area.

C. Try to hard reset the device by sliding the power button for 30-45 seconds then releasing the button then let the device reboot and see if you still have the issue.

D. Make sure your device is up to date on it's software. From the home screen hit Menu and then settings, on the bottom right of the screen you will see the Kindle version your device has. Check on www.amazon.com on the help pages to make sure you have the most updated software.

E. De-register and the re-register the Kindle then do a hard reset then let the device reboot and try to connect to your network. If you still have the issue. Go to a local place that providers free wifi and see if you can connect there to rule out if there is anything wrong with your connection at home or work.

F. Reset to factory Default but not recommended until you contact Kindle support so they can get information off the device in case further troubleshooting is needed.

Kindle Touch

Screen Issues

Device has a image stuck on the screen or lines running across or up and down the screen This could mean screen damaged that cant be fixed

Troubleshooting

A. Try to hard reset the device by sliding the power button for 30-45 seconds then releasing the button with the device unplug for the charger then let the device reboot and see if you still have the issue.

B. Try to hard reset the device by sliding the power button for 30-45 seconds then releasing the button with the device plug into the charger then let the device reboot and see if you still have the issue.

C. Make sure your device is up to date on it's software. From the home screen hit Menu and then settings, on the bottom right of the screen you will see the Kindle version your device has. Check on www.amazon.com on the help pages to make sure you have the most updated software.

D. If this does not fix your issue contact Kindle Support. 1-866-321-8851

Charging Issues

Device will not hold a charge or shows no signs of charging.

Troubleshooting

A. Try to hard reset the device by sliding the power button for 30-45 seconds then releasing the button with the device unplug for the charger then let the device reboot and see if you still have the issue.

B. Try to hard reset the device by sliding the power button for 30-45 seconds then releasing the button with the device plug into the charger then let the device reboot and see if you still have the issue.

C. Make sure your device is up to date on it's software. From the home screen hit Menu and then settings, on the bottom right of the screen you will see the Kindle version your device has. Check on www.amazon.com on the help pages to make sure you have the most updated software.

D. If this does not fix your issue contact Kindle Support. 1-866-321-8851

Downloading Issues

Books or purchases does not show up on your device.

A. Make sure your order has when through and it is paid for. Orders can be put into a pending status which can take up to 4 hours to clear. Also make sure you are purchasing the items on the correct account. Customers with multiple accounts can purchases item on the account their devices are not register too which they can not get the books onto their devices.

B. Make sure your device has a good connection where your purchases can download.

C. You can go and log on to your account at www.amazon.com and go to Manage Your Kindle and see if the purchase show up in your library and send it to your device from there.

D. Try to hard reset the device by sliding the power button for 30-45 seconds then releasing the button then let the device reboot and see if you still have the issue.

E. Make sure your device is up to date on it's software. From the home screen hit Menu and then settings, on the bottom right of the screen you will see the Kindle version your device has. Check on www.amazon.com on the help pages to make sure you have the most updated software.

F. If this does not fix your issue contact Kindle Support. 1-866-321-8851

Wireless Issues

If you device can not connect to a wireless network.

Troubleshooting

A. If you have difficulty connecting to the Kindle store or other wireless resources on your Kindle, make sure the wireless switch on the back of your Kindle 1st Generation is in the "ON" position and your battery is charged.

B. Make sure your network has a good connection Call your isp to make sure there is no outages in you area.

C. Try to hard reset the device by sliding the power button for 30-45 seconds then releasing the button then let the device reboot and see if you still have the issue.

D. Make sure your device is up to date on it's software. From the home screen hit Menu and then settings, on the bottom right of the screen you will see the Kindle version your device has. Check on www.amazon.com on the help pages to make sure you have the most updated software.

E. De-register and the re-register the Kindle then do a hard reset then let the device reboot and try to connect to your network. If you still have the issue. Go to a local place that providers free wifi and see if you can connect there to rule out if there is anything wrong with your connection at home or work.

F. Reset to factory Default but not recommended until you contact Kindle support so they can get information off the device in case further troubleshooting is needed. 1-866-321-8851

Kindle

Screen Issues

Device has a image stuck on the screen or lines running across or up and down the screen This could mean screen damaged that cant be fixed

Troubleshooting

A. Try to hard reset the device by pressing the power button for 30-45 seconds then releasing the button with the device unplug for the charger then let the device reboot and see if you still have the issue.

B. Try to hard reset the device by pressing the power button for 30-45 seconds then releasing the button with the device plug into the charger then let the device reboot and see if you still have the issue.

C. Make sure your device is up to date on it's software. From the home screen hit Menu and then settings, on the bottom right of the screen you will see the Kindle version your device has. Check on www.amazon.com on the help pages to make sure you have the most updated software.

D. If this does not fix your issue contact Kindle Support. 1-866-321-8851

Charging Issues

Device will not hold a charge or shows no signs of charging.

Troubleshooting

A. Try to hard reset the device by pressing the power button for 30-45 seconds then releasing the button with the device unplug for the charger then let the device reboot and see if you still have the issue.

B. Try to hard reset the device by pressing the power button for 30-45 seconds then releasing the button with the device plug into the charger then let the device reboot and see if you still have the issue.

C. Make sure your device is up to date on it's software. From the home screen hit Menu and then settings, on the bottom right of the screen you will see the Kindle version your device has. Check on www.amazon.com on the help pages to make sure you have the most updated software.

D. If this does not fix your issue contact Kindle Support. 1-866-321-8851

Downloading Issues

Books or purchases does not show up on your device.

A. Make sure your order has when through and it is paid for. Orders can be put into a pending status which can take up to 4 hours to clear. Also make sure you are purchasing the items on the correct account. Customers with multiple accounts can purchases item on the account their devices are not register too which they can not get the books onto their devices.

B. Make sure your device has a good connection where your purchases can download.

C. You can go and log on to your account at www.amazon.com and go to Manage Your Kindle and see if the purchase show up in your

library and send it to your device from there.

D. Try to hard reset the device by pressing the power button for 30-45 seconds then releasing the button then let the device reboot and see if you still have the issue.

E. Make sure your device is up to date on it's software. From the home screen hit Menu and then settings, on the bottom right of the screen you will see the Kindle version your device has. Check on www.amazon.com on the help pages to make sure you have the most updated software.

F. If this does not fix your issue contact Kindle Support. 1-866-321-8851

Wireless Issues

If you device can not connect to a wireless network.

Troubleshooting

A. If you have difficulty connecting to the Kindle store or other wireless resources on your Kindle, make sure the wireless switch on the back of your Kindle 1st Generation is in the "ON" position and your battery is charged.

B. Make sure your network has a good connection Call your isp to make sure there is no outages in you area.

C. Try to hard reset the device by pressing the power button for 30-45 seconds then releasing the button then let the device reboot and see if you still have the issue.

D. Make sure your device is up to date on it's software. From the home screen hit Menu and then settings, on the bottom right of the screen you will see the Kindle version your device has. Check on www.amazon.com on the help pages to make sure you have the most updated software.

E. De-register and the re-register the Kindle then do a hard reset then let the device reboot and try to connect to your network. If you still have the issue. Go to a local place that providers free wifi and see if you can connect there to rule out if there is anything wrong with your connection at home or work.

F. Reset to factory Default but not recommended until you contact Kindle support so they can get information off the device in case further troubleshooting is needed. 1-866-321-8851

Kindle Paper-White

Screen Issues

Device has a image stuck on the screen or lines running across or up and down the screen This could mean screen damaged that cant be fixed

Troubleshooting

A. Try to hard reset the device by pressing the power button for 30-45 seconds then releasing the button with the device unplug for the charger then let the device reboot and see if you still have the issue.

B. Try to hard reset the device by pressing the power button for 30-45 seconds then releasing the button with the device plug into the charger then let the device reboot and see if you still have the issue.

C. Make sure your device is up to date on it's software. From the home screen hit Menu and then settings, on the bottom right of the screen you will see the Kindle version your device has. Check on www.amazon.com on the help pages to make sure you have the most updated software.

D. If this does not fix your issue contact Kindle Support. 1-866-321-8851

Charging Issues

Device will not hold a charge or shows no signs of charging.

Troubleshooting

A. Try to hard reset the device by pressing the power button for 30-45 seconds then releasing the button with the device unplug for the charger then let the device reboot and see if you still have the issue.

B. Try to hard reset the device by pressing the power button for 30-45 seconds then releasing the button with the device plug into the charger then let the device reboot and see if you still have the issue.

C. Make sure your device is up to date on it's software. From the home screen hit Menu and then settings, on the bottom right of the screen you will see the Kindle version your device has. Check on www.amazon.com on the help pages to make sure you have the most updated software.

D. If this does not fix your issue contact Kindle Support. 1-866-321-8851

Downloading Issues

Books or purchases does not show up on your device.

A. Make sure your order has when through and it is paid for. Orders can be put into a pending status which can take up to 4 hours to clear. Also make sure you are purchasing the items on the correct account. Customers with multiple accounts can purchases item on the account their devices are not register too which they can not get the books onto their devices.

B. Make sure your device has a good connection where your purchases can download.

C. You can go and log on to your account at www.amazon.com and go to Manage Your Kindle and see if the purchase show up in your library and send it to your device from there.

D. Try to hard reset the device by pressing the power button for 30-45 seconds then releasing the button then let the device reboot and see if you still have the issue.

E. Make sure your device is up to date on it's software. From the home screen hit Menu and then settings, on the bottom right of the screen you will see the Kindle version your device has. Check on www.amazon.com on the help pages to make sure you have the most updated software.

F. If this does not fix your issue contact Kindle Support. 1-866-321-8851

Wireless Issues

If you device can not connect to a wireless network.

Troubleshooting

A. If you have difficulty connecting to the Kindle store or other wireless resources on your Kindle, make sure the wireless switch on the back of your Kindle 1st Generation is in the "ON" position and your battery is charged.

B. Make sure your network has a good connection Call your isp to make sure there is no outages in you area.

C. Try to hard reset the device by pressing the power button for 30-45 seconds then releasing the button then let the device reboot and see if you still have the issue.

D. Make sure your device is up to date on it's software.   From the home screen hit Menu and then settings, on the bottom right of the screen you will see the Kindle version your device has. Check on www.amazon.com on the help pages to make sure you have the most updated software.

E. De-register and the re-register the Kindle then do a hard reset then let the device reboot and try to connect to your network. If you still have the issue. Go to a local place that providers free wifi and see if you can connect there to rule out if there is anything wrong with your connection at home or work.

F. Reset to factory Default but not recommended until you contact Kindle support so they can get information off the device in case further troubleshooting is needed. 1-866-321-8851

Kindle Fire (1st Generation)

Screen Issues

Device has a image stuck on the screen or lines running across or up and down the screen This could mean screen damaged that cant be fixed

Troubleshooting

A. Try to hard reset the device by pressing the power button for 30-45 seconds then releasing the button with the device unplug for the charger then let the device reboot and see if you still have the issue.

B. Try to hard reset the device by pressing the power button for 30-45 seconds then releasing the button with the device plug into the charger then let the device reboot and see if you still have the issue.

C. Make sure your device is up to date on it's software.   From the home screen hit Menu and then settings, on the bottom right of the screen you will see the Kindle version your device has. Check on www.amazon.com on the help pages to make sure you have the most updated software.

D. If this does not fix your issue contact Kindle Support. 1-866-321-8851

Charging Issues

Device will not hold a charge or shows no signs of charging.

Troubleshooting

A. Try to hard reset the device by pressing the power button for 30-45 seconds then releasing the button with the device unplug for the charger then let the device reboot and see if you still have the issue.

B. Try to hard reset the device by pressing the power button for 30-45 seconds then releasing the button with the device plug into the charger then let the device reboot and see if you still have the issue.

C. Make sure your device is up to date on it's software. From the home screen hit Menu and then settings, on the bottom right of the screen you will see the Kindle version your device has. Check on www.amazon.com on the help pages to make sure you have the most updated software.

D. If this does not fix your issue contact Kindle Support. 1-866-321-8851

Downloading Issues

Books or purchases does not show up on your device.

A. Make sure your order has when through and it is paid for. Orders can be put into a pending status which can take up to 4 hours to clear. Also make sure you are purchasing the items on the correct account. Customers with multiple accounts can purchases item on the account their devices are not register too which they can not get the books onto their devices.

B. Make sure your device has a good connection where your purchases can download.

C. You can go and log on to your account at www.amazon.com and go to Manage Your Kindle and see if the purchase show up in your library and send it to your device from there.

D. Try to hard reset the device by pressing the power button for 30-45 seconds then releasing the button then let the device reboot and see if you still have the issue.

E. Make sure your device is up to date on it's software. From the home screen hit Menu and then settings, on the bottom right of the screen you will see the Kindle version your device has. Check on www.amazon.com on the help pages to make sure you have the most updated software.

F. If this does not fix your issue contact Kindle Support. 1-866-321-8851

Wireless Issues

If you device can not connect to a wireless network.

Troubleshooting

A. If you have difficulty connecting to the Kindle store or other wireless resources on your Kindle, make sure the wireless switch on the back of your Kindle 1st Generation is in the "ON" position and your battery is charged.

B. Make sure your network has a good connection Call your isp to make sure there is no outages in you area.

C. Try to hard reset the device by pressing the power button for 30-45 seconds then releasing the button then let the device reboot and see if you still have the issue.

D. Make sure your device is up to date on it's software. From the home screen hit Menu and then settings, on the bottom right of the screen you will see the Kindle version your device has. Check on www.amazon.com on the help pages to make sure you have the most updated software.

E. De-register and the re-register the Kindle then do a hard reset then let the device reboot and try to connect to your network. If you still have the issue. Go to a local place that providers free wifi and see if you can connect there to rule out if there is anything wrong with your connection

at home or work.

F. Reset to factory Default but not recommended until you contact Kindle support so they can get information off the device in case further troubleshooting is needed. 1-866-321-8851

Apps

Apps will not download or play correct or a error message appears.

A. Delete off the device and re download from the cloud.

B. Go into settings and the applications and filter by all applications. Click on Amazon app store and clear data and try to click on the app again from the home screen.

C. Find the app in your trying to play in application and clear data then click on the app again from the home screen

D. Try a hard reset on the device by pressing the power button for 30-45 seconds then releasing the button then let the device reboot and see if you still have the issue.

E. If this does not fix your issue call the App Store 1-866-749-7771

Web Issues

Troubleshooting

If your trying to use the web on your device but it will not work.

A. Click on the gear wheel on the top right next to the battery. Click more and go to application and filter by all application and go to Amazon browser and clear data. Go back to the home screen and click on web and see if your having the same issue.

B. Make sure your device is up to date on it's software.

C. De- register and re register the device. Then do a hard reset on the device by pressing the power button for 30-45 seconds then

releasing thebutton then let the device reboot and see if you still have the issue.

D. Reset to factory Default but not recommended until you contact Kindle support so they can get information off the device in case further troubleshooting is needed. 1-866-321-8851

Email Issue

If your having trouble not receiving your emails

Troubleshooting

A. Delete the email account off the device and re- enter it

B. Call you email provider to make sure you have the correct settings for their servers

C. If you call your email provider and you have the correct settings please call Kindle support 1-866-321-8851

Kindle Fire (2nd Generation)

Screen Issues

Device has a image stuck on the screen or lines running across or up and down the screen This could mean screen damaged that cant be fixed

Troubleshooting

A. Try to hard reset the device by pressing the power button for 30-45 seconds then releasing the button with the device unplug for the charger then let the device reboot and see if you still have the issue.

B. Try to hard reset the device by pressing the power button for 30-45 seconds then releasing the button with the device plug into the charger then let the device reboot and see if you still have the issue.

C. Make sure your device is up to date on it's software. From the home screen hit Menu and then settings, on the bottom right of the screen you will see the Kindle version your device has. Check on www.amazon.com on the help pages to make sure you have the most updated software.

D. If this does not fix your issue contact Kindle Support. 1-866-321-8851

Charging Issues

Device will not hold a charge or shows no signs of charging.

Troubleshooting

A. Try to hard reset the device by pressing the power button for 30-45 seconds then releasing the button with the device unplug for the charger then let the device reboot and see if you still have the issue.

B. Try to hard reset the device by pressing the power button for 30-45 seconds then releasing the button with the device plug into the charger then let the device reboot and see if you still have the issue.

C. Make sure your device is up to date on it's software. From the home screen hit Menu and then settings, on the bottom right of the screen you will see the Kindle version your device has. Check on www.amazon.com on the help pages to make sure you have the most updated software.

D. If this does not fix your issue contact Kindle Support. 1-866-321-8851

Downloading Issues

Books or purchases does not show up on your device.

A. Make sure your order has when through and it is paid for. Orders can be put into a pending status which can take up to 4 hours to clear. Also make sure you are purchasing the items on the correct account. Customers with multiple accounts can purchases item on the account their devices are not register too which they can not get the books onto their devices.

B. Make sure your device has a good connection where your purchases can download.

C. You can go and log on to your account at www.amazon.com and go to Manage Your Kindle and see if the purchase show up in your library and send it to your device from there.

D. Try to hard reset the device by pressing the power button for 30-45 seconds then releasing the button then let the device reboot and see if you still have the issue.

E. Make sure your device is up to date on it's software. From the home screen hit Menu and then settings, on the bottom right of the screen you will see the Kindle version your device has. Check on www.amazon.com on the help pages to make sure you have the most updated software.

F. If this does not fix your issue contact Kindle Support. 1-866-321-8851

Wireless Issues

If you device can not connect to a wireless network.

Troubleshooting

A. If you have difficulty connecting to the Kindle store or other wireless resources on your Kindle, make sure the wireless switch on the back of your Kindle 1st Generation is in the "ON" position and your battery is charged.

B. Make sure your network has a good connection Call your isp to make sure there is no outages in you area.

C. Try to hard reset the device by pressing the power button for 30-45 seconds then releasing the button then let the device reboot and see if you still have the issue.

D. Make sure your device is up to date on it's software.   From the home screen hit Menu and then settings, on the bottom right of the screen you will see the Kindle version your device has. Check on www.amazon.com on the help pages to make sure you have the most updated software.

E. De-register and the re-register the Kindle then do a hard reset then let the device reboot and try to connect to your network. If you still have the issue. Go to a local place that providers free wifi and see if you can connect there to rule out if there is anything wrong with your connection at home or work.

F. Reset to factory Default but not recommended until you contact Kindle support so they can get information off the device in case further troubleshooting is needed. 1-866-321-8851

Apps

Apps will not download or play correct or a error message appears.

Troubleshooting

A. Delete off the device and re download from the cloud.

B. Go into settings and the applications and filter by all applications. Click on Amazon app store and clear data and try to click on the app again from the home screen.

C. Find the app in your trying to play in application and clear data then click on the app again from the home screen

D. Try a hard reset on the device by pressing the power button for 30-45 seconds then releasing the button then let the device reboot and see if you still have the issue.

E. If this does not fix your issue call the App Store 1-866-749-7771

Web Issues

Toubleshooting

If your trying to use the web on your device but it will not work.

A. Click on the gear wheel on the top right next to the battery. Click more and go to application and filter by all application and go to Amazon

browser and clear data. Go back to the home screen and click on web and see if your having the same issue.

B. Make sure your device is up to date on it's software.

C. De- register and re register the device. Then do a hard reset on the device by pressing the power button for 30-45 seconds then releasing the button then let the device reboot and see if you still have the issue.

D. Reset to factory Default but not recommended until you contact Kindle support so they can get information off the device in case further troubleshooting is needed. 1-866-321-8851

Email Issue

If your having trouble not receiving your emails

Troubleshooting

A. Delete the email account off the device and re- enter it

B. Call you email provider to make sure you have the correct settings for their servers

C. If you call your email provider and you have the correct settings please call Kindle support
1-866-321-8851

Kindle Fire HD 7"

Screen Issues

Device has a image stuck on the screen or lines running across or up and down the screen This could mean screen damaged that cant be fixed

Troubleshooting

A. Try to hard reset the device by pressing the power button for 30-45 seconds then releasing the button with the device unplug for the charger then let the device reboot and see if you still have the issue.

B. Try to hard reset the device by pressing the power button for 30-45 seconds then releasing the button with the device plug into the charger then let the device reboot and see if you still have the issue.

C. Make sure your device is up to date on it's software. From the home screen hit Menu and then settings, on the bottom right of the screen you will see the Kindle version your device has. Check on www.amazon.com on the help pages to make sure you have the most updated software.

D. If this does not fix your issue contact Kindle Support. 1-866-321-8851

Charging Issues

Device will not hold a charge or shows no signs of charging.

Troubleshooting

A. Try to hard reset the device by pressing the power button for 30-45 seconds then releasing the button with the device unplug for the charger then let the device reboot and see if you still have the issue.

B. Try to hard reset the device by pressing the power button for 30-45 seconds then releasing the button with the device plug into the charger then let the device reboot and see if you still have the issue.

C. Make sure your device is up to date on it's software. From the home screen hit Menu and then settings, on the bottom right of the screen you will see the Kindle version your device has. Check on www.amazon.com on the help pages to make sure you have the most updated software.

D. If this does not fix your issue contact Kindle Support. 1-866-321-8851

Downloading Issues

Books or purchases does not show up on your device.

A. Make sure your order has when through and it is paid for. Orders can be put into a pending status which can take up to 4 hours to clear. Also make sure you are purchasing the items on the correct account. Customers with multiple accounts can purchases item on the account their devices are not register too which they can not get the books onto their devices.

B. Make sure your device has a good connection where your purchases can download.

C. You can go and log on to your account at www.amazon.com and go to Manage Your Kindle and see if the purchase show up in your library and send it to your device from there.

D. Try to hard reset the device by pressing the power button for 30-45 seconds then releasing the button then let the device reboot and see if you still have the issue.

E. Make sure your device is up to date on it's software. From the home screen hit Menu and then settings, on the bottom right of the screen you will see the Kindle version your device has. Check on www.amazon.com on the help pages to make sure you have the most updated software.

F. If this does not fix your issue contact Kindle Support. 1-866-321-8851

Wireless Issues

If you device can not connect to a wireless network.

Troubleshooting

A. If you have difficulty connecting to the Kindle store or other wireless resources on your Kindle, make sure the wireless switch on the back of your Kindle 1st Generation is in the "ON" position and your battery is charged.

B. Make sure your network has a good connection Call your isp to make sure there is no outages in you area.

C. Try to hard reset the device by pressing the power button for 30-45 seconds then releasing the button then let the device reboot and see if you still have the issue.

D. Make sure your device is up to date on it's software. From the home screen hit Menu and then settings, on the bottom right of the screen you will see the Kindle version your device has. Check on www.amazon.com on the help pages to make sure you have the most updated software.

E. De-register and the re-register the Kindle then do a hard reset then let the device reboot and try to connect to your network. If you still have the issue. Go to a local place that providers free wifi and see if you can connect there to rule out if there is anything wrong with your connection at home or work.

F. Reset to factory Default but not recommended until you contact Kindle support so they can get information off the device in case further troubleshooting is needed. 1-866-321-8851

Apps

Apps will not download or play correct or a error message appears.

Troubleshooting

A. Delete off the device and re download from the cloud.

B. Go into settings and the applications and filter by all applications. Click on Amazon app store and clear data and try to click on the app again from the home screen.

C. Find the app in your trying to play in application and clear data then click on the app again from the home screen

D. Try a hard reset on the device by pressing the power button for 30-45 seconds then releasing the button then let the device reboot and see if you still have the issue.

E. If this does not fix your issue call the App Store 1-866-749-7771

Web Issues

Troubleshooting

If your trying to use the web on your device but it will not work.

A. Click on the gear wheel on the top right next to the battery. Click more and go to application and filter by all application and go to Amazon browser and clear data. Go back to the home screen and click on web and see if your having the same issue.

B. Make sure your device is up to date on it's software.

C. De- register and re register the device. Then do a hard reset on the device by pressing the power button for 30-45 seconds then releasing the button then let the device reboot and see if you still have the issue.

D. Reset to factory Default but not recommended until you contact Kindle support so they can get information off the device in case further troubleshooting is needed. 1-866-321-8851

Email Issue

If your having trouble not receiving your emails

Troubleshooting

A. Delete the email account off the device and re- enter it

B. Call you email provider to make sure you have the correct settings for their servers

C. If you call your email provider and you have the correct settings please call Kindle support
1-866-321-8851

Kindle Fire HD 8.9

Screen Issues

Device has a image stuck on the screen or lines running across or up and down the screen This could mean screen damaged that cant be fixed

Troubleshooting

A. Try to hard reset the device by pressing the power button for 30-45 seconds then releasing the button with the device unplug for the charger then let the device reboot and see if you still have the issue.

B. Try to hard reset the device by pressing the power button for 30-45 seconds then releasing the button with the device plug into the charger then let the device reboot and see if you still have the issue.

C. Make sure your device is up to date on it's software. From the home screen hit Menu and then settings, on the bottom right of the screen you will see the Kindle version your device has. Check on www.amazon.com on the help pages to make sure you have the most updated software.

D. If this does not fix your issue contact Kindle Support. 1-866-321-8851

Charging Issues

Device will not hold a charge or shows no signs of charging.

Troubleshooting

A. Try to hard reset the device by pressing the power button for 30-45 seconds then releasing the button with the device unplug for the charger then let the device reboot and see if you still have the issue.

B. Try to hard reset the device by pressing the power button for 30-45 seconds then releasing the button with the device plug into the charger then let the device reboot and see if you still have the issue.

C. Make sure your device is up to date on it's software. From the home screen hit Menu and then settings, on the bottom right of the screen you will see the Kindle version your device has. Check on www.amazon.com on the help pages to make sure you have the most updated software.

D. If this does not fix your issue contact Kindle Support. 1-866-321-8851

Downloading Issues

Books or purchases does not show up on your device.

A. Make sure your order has when through and it is paid for. Orders can be put into a pending status which can take up to 4 hours to clear. Also make sure you are purchasing the items on the correct account. Customers with multiple accounts can purchases item on the account their devices are not register too which they can not get the books onto their devices.

B. Make sure your device has a good connection where your purchases can download.

C. You can go and log on to your account at www.amazon.com and go to Manage Your Kindle and see if the purchase show up in your library and send it to your device from there.

D. Try to hard reset the device by pressing the power button for 30-45 seconds then releasing the button then let the device reboot and see if you still have the issue.

E. Make sure your device is up to date on it's software. From the home screen hit Menu and then settings, on the bottom right of the screen you will see the Kindle version your device has. Check on www.amazon.com on the help pages to make sure you have the most updated software.

F. If this does not fix your issue contact Kindle Support. 1-866-321-8851

Wireless Issues

If you device can not connect to a wireless network.

Troubleshooting

A. If you have difficulty connecting to the Kindle store or other wireless resources on your Kindle, make sure the wireless switch on the back of your Kindle 1st Generation is in the "ON" position and your battery is charged.

B. Make sure your network has a good connection Call your isp to make sure there is no outages in you area.

C. Try to hard reset the device by pressing the power button for 30-45 seconds then releasing the button then let the device reboot and see if you still have the issue.

D. Make sure your device is up to date on it's software. From the home screen hit Menu and then settings, on the bottom right of the screen you will see the Kindle version your device has. Check on www.amazon.com on the help pages to make sure you have the most updated software.

E. De-register and the re-register the Kindle then do a hard reset then let the device reboot and try to connect to your network. If you still have the issue. Go to a local place that providers free wifi and see if you can connect there to rule out if there is anything wrong with your connection at home or work.

F. Reset to factory Default but not recommended until you contact Kindle support so they can get information off the device in case further troubleshooting is needed.
1-866-321-8851

Apps

Apps will not download or play correct or a error message appears.

Troubleshooting

A. Delete off the device and re download from the cloud.

B. Go into settings and the applications and filter by all applications. Click on Amazon app store and clear data and try to click on the app again from the home screen.

C. Find the app in your trying to play in application and clear data then click on the app again from the home screen

D. Try a hard reset on the device by pressing the power button for 30-45 seconds then releasing the button then let the device reboot and see if you still have the issue.

E. If this does not fix your issue call the App Store 1-866-749-7771

Web Issues

Troubleshooting

If your trying to use the web on your device but it will not work.

A. Click on the gear wheel on the top right next to the battery. Click more and go to application and filter by all application and go to Amazon browser and clear data. Go back to the home screen and click on web and see if your having the same issue.

B. Make sure your device is up to date on it's software.

C. De- register and re register the device. Then do a hard reset on the device by pressing the power button for

30-45 seconds then releasing the button then let the device reboot and see if you still have the issue.

D. Reset to factory Default but not recommended until you contact Kindle support so they can get information off the device in case further troubleshooting is needed.
1-866-321-8851

Email Issue

If your having trouble not receiving your emails

Troubleshooting

A. Delete the email account off the device and re- enter it

B. Call you email provider to make sure you have the correct settings for their servers

C. If you call your email provider and you have the correct settings please call Kindle support
1-866-321-8851

A few new features that's on the new Kindle fire HDX are.

1.The all new mayday button. You can get a live Amazon tech on your screen in 15 seconds or less. You must be connected to a wifi before you can use this service.

2.The on and off button and the volume buttons are on the back sides of the device and clearly marked.

Kindle Fire HDX 7"

Screen Issues

Device has a image stuck on the screen or lines running across or up and down the screen This could mean screen damaged that cant be fixed

Troubleshooting

A. Try to hard reset the device by pressing the power button for 30-45 seconds then releasing the button with the device unplug for the charger then let the device reboot and see if you still have the issue.

B. Try to hard reset the device by pressing the power button for 30-45 seconds then releasing the button with the device plug into the charger then let the device reboot and see if you still have the issue.

C. Make sure your device is up to date on it's software. From the home screen hit Menu and then settings, on the bottom right of the screen you will see the Kindle version your device has. Check on www.amazon.com on the help pages to make sure you have the most updated software.

D. If this does not fix your issue contact Kindle Support. 1-866-321-8851

Charging Issues

Device will not hold a charge or shows no signs of charging.

Troubleshooting

A. Try to hard reset the device by pressing the power button for 30-45 seconds then releasing the button with the device unplug for the charger then let the device reboot and see if you still have the issue.

B. Try to hard reset the device by pressing the power button for 30-45 seconds then releasing the button with the device plug into the charger then let the device reboot and see if you still have the issue.

C. Make sure your device is up to date on it's software. From the home screen hit Menu and then settings, on the bottom right of the screen you will see the Kindle version your device has. Check on www.amazon.com on the help pages to make sure you have the most updated software.

D. If this does not fix your issue contact Kindle Support. 1-866-321-8851

Downloading Issues

Books or purchases does not show up on your device.

A. Make sure your order has when through and it is paid for. Orders can be put into a pending status which can take up to 4 hours to clear. Also make sure you are purchasing the items on the correct account. Customers with multiple accounts can purchases item on the account their devices are not register too which they can not get the books onto their devices.

B. Make sure your device has a good connection where your purchases can download.

C. You can go and log on to your account at www.amazon.com and go to Manage Your Kindle and see if the purchase show up in your library and send it to your device from there.

D. Try to hard reset the device by pressing the power button for 30-45 seconds then releasing the button then let the device reboot and see if you still have the issue.

E. Make sure your device is up to date on it's software. From the home screen hit Menu and then settings, on the bottom right of the screen you will see the Kindle version your device has. Check on www.amazon.com on the help pages to make sure you have the most updated software.

F. If this does not fix your issue contact Kindle Support. 1-866-321-8851

Wireless Issues

If you device can not connect to a wireless network.

Troubleshooting

A. If you have difficulty connecting to the Kindle store or other wireless resources on your Kindle, make sure the wireless switch on the back of your Kindle 1st Generation is in the "ON" position and your battery is charged.

B. Make sure your network has a good connection Call your isp to make sure there is no outages in you area.

C. Try to hard reset the device by pressing the power button for 30-45 seconds then releasing the button then let the device reboot and see if you still have the issue.

D. Make sure your device is up to date on it's software. From the home screen hit Menu and then settings, on the bottom right of the screen you will see the Kindle version your device has. Check on www.amazon.com on the help pages to make sure you have the most updated software.

E. De-register and the re-register the Kindle then do a hard reset then let the device reboot and try to connect to your network. If you still have the issue. Go to a local place that providers free wifi and see if you can connect there to rule out if there is anything wrong with your connection at home or work.

F. Reset to factory Default but not recommended until you contact Kindle support so they can get information off the device in case further troubleshooting is needed. 1-866-321-8851

Apps

Apps will not download or play correct or a error message appears.

30-45 seconds then releasing the button then let the device reboot and see if you still have the issue.

D. Reset to factory Default but not recommended until you contact Kindle support so they can get information off the device in case further troubleshooting is needed.
1-866-321-8851

Email Issue

If your having trouble not receiving your emails

Troubleshooting

A. Delete the email account off the device and re- enter it

B. Call you email provider to make sure you have the correct settings for their servers

C. If you call your email provider and you have the correct settings please call Kindle support
1-866-321-8851

A few new features that's on the new Kindle fire HDX are.

1.The all new mayday button. You can get a live Amazon tech on your screen in 15 seconds or less. You must be connected to a wifi before you can use this service.

2.The on and off button and the volume buttons are on the back sides of the device and clearly marked.

Kindle Fire HDX 7"

Screen Issues

Device has a image stuck on the screen or lines running across or up and down the screen This could mean screen damaged that cant be fixed

Troubleshooting

A. Try to hard reset the device by pressing the power button for 30-45 seconds then releasing the button with the device unplug for the charger then let the device reboot and see if you still have the issue.

B. Try to hard reset the device by pressing the power button for 30-45 seconds then releasing the button with the device plug into the charger then let the device reboot and see if you still have the issue.

C. Make sure your device is up to date on it's software. From the home screen hit Menu and then settings, on the bottom right of the screen you will see the Kindle version your device has. Check on www.amazon.com on the help pages to make sure you have the most updated software.

D. If this does not fix your issue contact Kindle Support. 1-866-321-8851

Charging Issues

Device will not hold a charge or shows no signs of charging.

Troubleshooting

A. Try to hard reset the device by pressing the power button for 30-45 seconds then releasing the button with the device unplug for the charger then let the device reboot and see if you still have the issue.

B. Try to hard reset the device by pressing the power button for 30-45 seconds then releasing the button with the device plug into the charger then let the device reboot and see if you still have the issue.

C. Make sure your device is up to date on it's software. From the home screen hit Menu and then settings, on the bottom right of the screen you will see the Kindle version your device has. Check on www.amazon.com on the help pages to make sure you have the most updated software.

D. If this does not fix your issue contact Kindle Support. 1-866-321-8851

Downloading Issues

Books or purchases does not show up on your device.

A. Make sure your order has when through and it is paid for. Orders can be put into a pending status which can take up to 4 hours to clear. Also make sure you are purchasing the items on the correct account. Customers with multiple accounts can purchases item on the account their devices are not register too which they can not get the books onto their devices.

B. Make sure your device has a good connection where your purchases can download.

C. You can go and log on to your account at www.amazon.com and go to Manage Your Kindle and see if the purchase show up in your library and send it to your device from there.

D. Try to hard reset the device by pressing the power button for 30-45 seconds then releasing the button then let the device reboot and see if you still have the issue.

E. Make sure your device is up to date on it's software. From the home screen hit Menu and then settings, on the bottom right of the screen you will see the Kindle version your device has. Check on www.amazon.com on the help pages to make sure you have the most updated software.

F. If this does not fix your issue contact Kindle Support. 1-866-321-8851

Wireless Issues

If you device can not connect to a wireless network.

Troubleshooting

A. If you have difficulty connecting to the Kindle store or other wireless resources on your Kindle, make sure the wireless switch on the back of your Kindle 1st Generation is in the "ON" position and your battery is charged.

B. Make sure your network has a good connection Call your isp to make sure there is no outages in you area.

C. Try to hard reset the device by pressing the power button for 30-45 seconds then releasing the button then let the device reboot and see if you still have the issue.

D. Make sure your device is up to date on it's software. From the home screen hit Menu and then settings, on the bottom right of the screen you will see the Kindle version your device has. Check on www.amazon.com on the help pages to make sure you have the most updated software.

E. De-register and the re-register the Kindle then do a hard reset then let the device reboot and try to connect to your network. If you still have the issue. Go to a local place that providers free wifi and see if you can connect there to rule out if there is anything wrong with your connection at home or work.

F. Reset to factory Default but not recommended until you contact Kindle support so they can get information off the device in case further troubleshooting is needed. 1-866-321-8851

Apps

Apps will not download or play correct or a error message appears.

A. Delete off the device and re download from the cloud.

B. Go into settings and the applications and filter by all applications. Click on Amazon app store and clear data and try to click on the app again from the home screen.

C. Find the app in your trying to play in application and clear data then click on the app again from the home screen

D. Try a hard reset on the device by pressing the power button for 30-45 seconds then releasing the button then let the device reboot and see if you still have the issue.

E. If this does not fix your issue call the App Store 1-866-749-7771

Web Issues

If your trying to use the web on your device but it will not work.

A. Click on the gear wheel on the top right next to the battery. Click more and go to application and filter by all application and go to Amazon browser and clear data. Go back to the home screen and click on web and see if your having the same issue.

B. Make sure your device is up to date on it's software.

C. De- register and re register the device. Then do a hard reset on the device by pressing the power button for 30-45 seconds then releasing the button then let the device reboot and see if you still have the issue.

D.   Reset to factory Default but not recommended until you contact Kindle support so they can get information off the device in case

further troubleshooting is needed. 1-866-321-8851

Email Issue

If your having trouble not receiving your emails

A. Delete the email account off the device and re- enter it

B. Call you email provider to make sure you have the correct settings for their servers

C. If you call your email provider and you have the correct settings please call Kindle support 1-866-321-8851

Kindle Fire HDX 8.9"

Screen Issues

Device has a image stuck on the screen or lines running across or up and down the screen This could mean screen damaged that cant be fixed

A. Try to hard reset the device by pressing the power button for 30-45 seconds then releasing the button with the device unplug for the charger then let the device reboot and see if you still have the issue.

B. Try to hard reset the device by pressing the power button for 30-45 seconds then releasing the button with the device plug into the charger then let the device reboot and see if you still have the issue.

C. Make sure your device is up to date on it's software. From the home screen hit Menu and then settings, on the bottom right of the

screen youwill see the Kindle version your device has. Check on www.amazon.com on the help pages to make sure you have the most updated software.

D. If this does not fix your issue contact Kindle Support. 1-866-321-8851

Charging Issues

Device will not hold a charge or shows no signs of charging.

Troubleshooting

A. Try to hard reset the device by pressing the power button for 30-45 seconds then releasing the button with the device unplug for the charger then let the device reboot and see if you still have the issue.

B. Try to hard reset the device by pressing the power button for 30-45 seconds then releasing the button with the device plug into the charger then let the device reboot and see if you still have the issue.

C. Make sure your device is up to date on it's software. From the home screen hit Menu and then settings, on the bottom right of the screen you will see the Kindle version your device has. Check on www.amazon.com on the help pages to make sure you have the most updated software.

D. If this does not fix your issue contact Kindle Support. 1-866-321-8851

Downloading Issues

Books or purchases does not show up on your device.

A. Make sure your order has when through and it is paid for. Orders can be put into a pending status which can take up to 4 hours to clear. Also make sure you are purchasing the items on the correct account. Customers with multiple accounts can purchases item on the account their devices are not register too which they can not get the books onto their devices.

B. Make sure your device has a good connection where your purchases can download.

C. You can go and log on to your account at www.amazon.com and go to Manage Your Kindle and see if the purchase show up in your library and send it to your device from there.

D. Try to hard reset the device by pressing the power button for 30-45 seconds then releasing the button then let the device reboot and see if you still have the issue.

E. Make sure your device is up to date on it's software. From the home screen hit Menu and then settings, on the bottom right of the screen you will see the Kindle version your device has. Check on www.amazon.com on the help pages to make sure you have the most updated software.

F. If this does not fix your issue contact Kindle Support. 1-866-321-8851

Wireless Issues

If you device can not connect to a wireless network.

Troubleshooting

A. If you have difficulty connecting to the Kindle store or other wireless resources on your Kindle, make sure the wireless switch on the back of your Kindle 1st Generation is in the "ON" position and your battery is charged.

B. Make sure your network has a good connection Call your isp to make sure there is no outages in you area.

C. Try to hard reset the device by pressing the power button for 30-45 seconds then releasing the button then let the device reboot and see if you still have the issue.

D. Make sure your device is up to date on it's software. From the home screen hit Menu and then settings, on the bottom right of the screen you will see the Kindle version your device has. Check on www.amazon.com on the help pages to make sure you have the most updated software.

E. De-register and the re-register the Kindle then do a hard reset then let the device reboot and try to connect to your network. If you still have the issue. Go to a local place that providers free wifi and see if you can connect there to rule out if there is anything wrong with your connection at home or work.

F. Reset to factory Default but not recommended until you contact Kindle support so they can get information off the device in case further troubleshooting is needed. 1-866-321-8851

Apps

Apps will not download or play correct or a error message appears.

Troubleshooting

A. Delete off the device and re download from the cloud.

B. Go into settings and the applications and filter by all applications. Click on Amazon app store and clear data and try to click on the app again from the home screen.

C. Find the app in your trying to play in application and clear data then click on the app again from the home screen

D. Try a hard reset on the device by pressing the power button for 30-45 seconds then releasing the button then let the device reboot and see if you still have the issue.

E. If this does not fix your issue call the App Store 1-866-749-7771

Web Issues

Troubleshooting

If your trying to use the web on your device but it will not work.

A. Click on the gear wheel on the top right next to the battery. Click more and go to application and filter by all application and go to Amazon browser and clear data. Go back to the home screen and click on web and see if your having the same issue.

B. Make sure your device is up to date on it's software.

C. De- register and re register the device. Then do a hard reset on the device by pressing the power button for 30-45 seconds then releasing the button then let the device reboot and see if you still have the issue.

D. Reset to factory Default but not recommended until you contact Kindle support so they can get information off the device in case further troubleshooting is needed. 1-866-321-8851

Email Issue

If your having trouble not receiving your emails

Troubleshooting

A. Delete the email account off the device and re- enter it

B. Call you email provider to make sure you have the correct settings for their servers

C. If you call your email provider and you have the correct settings please call Kindle support
1-866-321-8851

Notes

Notes